Your Journey to Spiritual Maturity
Volume I – The Fool

Your Journey to Spiritual Maturity
Volume I – The Fool

Rev. R. D. Bernard

Your Journey to Spiritual Maturity
Volume I – The Fool

Copyright © 2010 by Reginald Bernard

All rights reserved. No part of this book may be used or reproduced by any means, graphic, electronic, or mechanical, including photocopying, recording, taping or by any information storage retrieval system without the written permission of the publisher except in the case of brief quotations embodied in critical articles and reviews.

The views expressed in this work are solely those of the author and do not necessarily reflect the views of the publisher, and the publisher hereby disclaims any responsibility for them.

ISBN: 978-0-615-36943-3

Printed in the United States of America

To the members and friends of the
King Solomon Baptist Church
Vicksburg, Mississippi

Contents

Foreword……………………………………….....2

Chapter 1   Who in Hell Is Praying for You?.................3

Chapter 2   The Ghetto Gospel……………………….17

Chapter 3   What Happens to the Family When the Mother Talks to a Snake?..........................28

Chapter 4   What Happens to the Family When the Father is Absent?...41

Chapter 5   When Wrong Seems Right………………56

Chapter 6   What Will It Take For You to Repent?......67

Reflections……………………………………..........78

Self Study……………………………………….....80

Foreword

There is a need for serious writing in the Baptist tradition from the African-American perspective. Rev. R.D. Bernard, who pastors in the heart of the inner-city South, has answered the call with his previous book, **Making Church Matter** and **Volume I** of **Your Journey to Spiritual Maturity – The Fool.** This present volume speaks to a need in our churches, our schools, and indeed, every facet of our community. The issues it addresses will be readily recognizable to anyone who has spent time in our communities.

Pastor Bernard masterfully blends Scripture and life in his ministry at the King Solomon Baptist Church and it is evident in **Your Journey to Spiritual Maturity – Volume I – The Fool.** This book should be required reading in every New Member's Orientation class.

Dr. Jesse Horton, Pastor
Emmanuel Baptist Church
Jackson, Mississippi
June 2010

1

Who in Hell is Praying for You?

Luke 16:19-31 – *There was a certain rich man, which was clothed in purple and fine linen, and fared sumptuously every day:*
And there was a certain beggar named Lazarus, which was laid at his gate, full of sores,
And desiring to be fed with the crumbs which fell from the rich man's table: moreover the dogs came and licked his sores.
And it came to pass, that the beggar died, and was carried by the angels into Abraham's bosom: the rich man also died, and was buried;
And in hell he lifted up his eyes, being in torments, and seeth Abraham afar off, and Lazarus in his bosom.
And he cried and said, Father Abraham, have mercy on me, and send Lazarus, that he may dip the tip of his finger in water, and cool my tongue; for I am tormented in this flame.
But Abraham said, Son, remember that thou in thy lifetime receivedst thy good things, and likewise Lazarus evil things: but now he is comforted, and thou art tormented.
And beside all this, between us and you there is a great gulf fixed: so that they which would pass from hence to you cannot; neither can they pass to us, that would come from thence.
Then he said, I pray thee therefore, father, that thou wouldst send him to my father's house:
For I have five brethren; that he may testify unto them, lest they also come into this place of torment.
Abraham saith unto him, They have Moses and the prophets; let them hear them.
And he said, Nay, father Abraham: but if one went unto them from the dead, they will repent.
And he said unto him, If they hear not Moses and the prophets, neither will they be persuaded, though one rose from the dead.

Kristen was a mess. The sad part was that she didn't even know it. She had been my friend my whole life and I knew she wasn't saved. "Tammie, I don't know why you keep inviting me to your church. I go to church." Kristen just didn't get it. "Kristen, you have to surrender and live a holy life," I replied sounding like a broken record. "Ain't nothing special about your church," she snapped. "You know, my grandfather pastored our church. I know I'm saved and I know about the Bible." "Look at the lifestyles of people around you, girl! I know you see all the adultery and fornication, right there in the church," I replied passionately.

I knew it was now or never for Kristen. I had to expose the great big lie in her spiritual life. "Be careful Tammie – you are talking about my family. Are you trying to tell me that my dead grandfather, the former pastor, didn't go to Heaven?"

Kristen thought she had me, but I said, "Let's go to the Scriptures and let God do the talking. Let's start with Luke 16:19-31." Kristen agreed reluctantly. Through much nurturing and prayer, she eventually surrendered to God.

The great contradiction of 21st century church life is that we seem to have the unspoken belief that there is not a Hell. Of course, if we were to take a survey today, you would all assure me that there *is* a Hell. Yet, if I also asked, "Are you going there?" you would undoubtedly tell me "*no*." But if I judged, not by what you told me, but by your actions – then there would be a great contradiction. My desire is not to make you upset, but to help you to hear the voices that are calling from beyond the grave.

The great majority of church members in this land and country would state affirmatively that there is definitely a Hell. In all likelihood, they would state with equal vigor that they themselves would **not** spend eternity there. In reality, we know with a reasonable certainty that Hell will be inhabited by some of us because of our behavior.

The same Bible that speaks so glowingly of mansions and streets of gold in a place called *"Heaven,"* also speaks just as definitively of a place of eternal torment, where a flame does not cease to burn the body and yet not consume it. This place is called *"Hell"* or *Hades* in the Greek and the Bible unashamedly proclaims its existence.

Now I know that some highly educated and enlightened persons would say that I am insulting your intelligence. Perhaps they would make the argument that Hell is not really a literal place. "After all," they may reason, "people who are near death don't talk about flames; they talk about 'going to the light.'" To this argument I would respond by saying that these people don't know whom the source of *that* light is. 2nd Corinthians 11:14 reads, *"And no marvel; for Satan himself is transformed into an angel of light."*

I would also say that if Hell is not a literal place, then neither is its polar opposite - Heaven. So, if we want to indeed spend eternity with the Lord, we must also acknowledge that there is a possibility that some of us may spend eternity in Hell. Quite simply, the one place does not exist without the other.

I know some other very sympathetic person is thinking that a God of love would not send a person to Hell. I would respond to anyone who believes that Hell is not real by saying that if Hell is not real – then Christ Himself is not real - for Christ speaks of Hell more than any other person in Scripture. It wasn't Satan who created Hell – it was God. It is precisely *because* God loves us that He warns us so much about Hell.

The passage under our consideration is one such passage in which Christ warns us about Hell and how not to end up there. He allows us to see into the inner workings of Hell and to experience Hell from the perspective of a man who earned the right to go there. The thing that immediately stands out to me in this passage is its suddenness.

Understand that some of us will be caught off guard much like the rich man, who closed his physical eyes in death, then opened his spiritual eyes and found himself in Hell. Verse 23 reads that *"...in Hell he lifted up his eyes..."* The reality of Hell is pictured as being sudden and immediate. When a person dies outside of Christ, they are immediately in torments.

If for the Christian, 2nd Corinthians 5:8 reads *"to be absent from the body, and to be present with the*

Lord," then we may reasonably surmise that for the unbeliever *"to be absent from the body is to be away from the Lord – in Hell."* I know that it is not pleasant to be addressed about going to Hell. Far be it from me to suggest that any of my readers are going to Hell.

So I don't want to focus necessarily on you, I would like for you to think about *others* who have gone on before you. This passage of Scripture from our human perspective is really about them and what they may be doing at this very moment. Christ is allowing the dead to speak one last time to us.

Their message leads one to believe that there are only two possible conditions that their souls can be in – one is a state of rest and the other is a state of torment. One resides in the bosom of Abraham and the other resides in the flames of Hell. Now the balance of this passage is not given to the person who resides in Heaven, or in the bosom of Abraham. The majority of the attention is focused on the man who died and went to Hell.

If we were to think closely about all of the people we have known who are now deceased, we must know of some that we were close to and who loved us, but who probably didn't make it to Heaven. It is their testimony that this passage is concerned with, for they undoubtedly would be in Hell praying for you.

Such was the case with this *"certain rich man."* His name is not provided, so we know right off the bat that this man could represent any one of our relatives who died and was not saved. The chance to be saved is closed at death. This is why all the old preachers would say: "Come while the blood is running warm in your veins."

After death, there is no chance for a person to be saved or delivered from the torments of Hell. The door to salvation, eternal bliss and those heavenly mansions is closed permanently when we shut our physical eyes for the last time without being saved.

There are certain things that only become clear to us *after* we die. The sad part about this is that many of us will not learn that God was not pleased with our lives until *after* we die. Of course, it's too late to do anything about it then. Sadly, some will learn for a certainty that Hell is real *after* they die.

Our true estate and our true spiritual condition are not made manifest until after we die. Undoubtedly if this man had known in life what he knew in death, he would have lived a very different life. Right now, many of us know that we are not living right, but we refuse to change direction because we either believe there is no Hell; that we will have time to repent, or even that we somehow are not going to Hell. My advice to you is not to get caught off guard and be surprised at how sudden one can find themselves in Hell.

After the rich man realizes that there is no salvation after death and that his torment is permanent, his thoughts turned to his five brothers. We are not told much about these brothers, but we can surmise several things. First of all, we know that they are still living, for the way to salvation and Heaven closes at death.

Secondly, we may surmise that they were living lives similar to the one this man lived. If they were living lives that would have gotten them into Heaven or Abraham's bosom, then there would be no need to warn them. Thirdly, these men admired their rich brother. In fact, they probably followed the pattern he laid down in his life. Yet, what the five brothers didn't know and what the rich man wants to warn them about is that he would do it differently if he could do it all over again. In other words, the deceased brother would have repented before he died.

We admire and love many people for the life they lived. Some of these people are in Hell right now wishing they could tell us *not* to admire them or their lifestyles. Those who are in Hell see things differently than they did when they were on earth. If we could hear the voices from the graves, some of them would be telling us to change our ways because Hell is no joke.

Since we can't literally hear their voices, let us take the testimony of this unnamed man who really represents every person who is in Hell's torments. This man, like some of our relatives, prayed a prayer in verses 27 and 28. The form of the word "*pray*" used in the Greek is erotao, and it means "to ask, to beseech, to inquire or to desire."

This unnamed man, who could be our father, brother or uncle, prayed that God would send someone from the dead to warn us about Hell. In life, this brother was probably the model church member – a deacon perhaps. He didn't get sent to Hell because he didn't come to church. This man was probably a Jew. Jews were the covenant people of God – much like today's Christians. The Jews practically lived in church. You should know that going to church and serving, as an officer will not save you from Hell; only loving Christ and treating your neighbor as yourself will keep you from Hell.

Additionally, this man had probably been circumcised and observed the ritual laws incumbent on being a Jew. In today's Christian terms, he probably had been baptized and confessed Christ. You need to know that just because you were baptized does not mean that you get a free ticket to Heaven. Water Baptism does not save you – but Baptism by the Holy Spirit does.

John the Baptist told his congregation down by the Jordan River that *"I indeed baptize you with water; but One mightier than I cometh, the latchet of whose shoes I am not worthy to unloose: He shall baptize you with the Holy Ghost and with fire."*[1] Water washes the outside; it doesn't touch the inside. The Holy Ghost washes the inside and changes us from the inside out. The Holy Spirit is the one who ushers in the new birth. If you have not experienced the new birth, you cannot go to Heaven. Jesus told Nicodemus, *"Marvel not that I said unto thee,*

Ye must be born again."[2] We have to be changed by the renewing power of the Holy Spirit if we want our names written in the Lamb's Book of Life.

This man in Hell was also very rich, which the Jews thought was a sign that a person had favor with God. This belief arose because the great patriarch of the faith, Father Abraham, was very rich. So this man was, in his own mind and in the mind of his community, "blessed and highly favored."

The problem with this man's life is that he realized too late that he had become an idol and a stumbling block to his brothers. No doubt they looked up to him and patterned themselves after him. We, too, in the Baptist church look up to our relatives and ancestors, and we honor them and quote them every chance we get.

Sometimes Satan allows us to put people up on pedestals, so that we will be more concerned with what *they* said and what *they* did – rather than what *God* is saying and what *God* wants us to do. Did you not know that many pastors are still pastoring from the grave? Hopefully, you know that many church leaders are still leading our churches from the grave.

Why is it so hard for us to realize that some of our relatives and loved ones may not have made it to Heaven? When I hold up the Bible against their lives, I see a great contradiction. How can we say that Brother Smith who raised so much hell when he was living is now in Heaven? How can we say that Sister Smith, who served on the Mother Board, is in Heaven when she hurt so many people on Earth?

As a Pastor, I hurt sometimes because I have to challenge assumptions and beliefs. We can never put people up too high. We can never put their traditions alongside Scripture. The two just are not equal. We have the testimony of this unnamed man who *knew* he had led some of his loved ones the wrong way when he was alive. He didn't want all five of his brothers to end up in Hell with him.

Of all the folks who have passed through your life, who could be in Hell right now wishing they could warn you? Who is in Hell right now wishing that you would change your ways? I know we like to think pleasant thoughts about the dead. We say things like "they are no longer suffering" or "they are gone to a better place."

We say these things even though they may be outright lies. If you are in Hell, you *will* suffer and it's not a better place – it's a worse place. There are many there who may still love us. They don't want us to make the same mistakes that they did, or we too, will end up in Hell praying for our children.

What did the man want to warn His brothers about? He wanted to warn them to change their behavior toward one another. It was because of the rich man's behavior toward his neighbor that God gave him a one-way ticket to Hell. Understand, we can say that we are saved, sanctified and Holy Ghost filled all day long, but we still have an obligation to our neighbor.

The Lord said in Matthew 19:19 "...*Thou shalt love thy neighbour as thyself.*" The rich man worried, not about the poor beggar who was laid at his gate, but about himself and *his* family. We seem to be content to keep up the fussing and feuding in our families and in our churches as if we don't have to meet God face to face.

Within our families, we play favorites and we also have "black sheep." We have outside children that we will not even acknowledge and for whom we will not take responsibility. Church folk especially act as if we don't know the difference between right and wrong. We try to keep up appearances even when we know that we are dead wrong.

God wants you to know today, that this is what the rich man was sent to Hell for – he would not acknowledge his brother. Your dead relative who used to do this very *same* thing is praying for you to repent. He doesn't want you to be like him anymore – you need a change.

In our community, if one family gets a few more dollars than another family, then all of sudden they start looking down on everybody else. The beggar was laid at the gate of the rich man and he had to look down on him as he passed him every morning.

I know that some of us have been taught to only associate with a certain class of people. I want to warn you that whoever taught you this lesson is probably in Hell right now regretting it. They are praying that you will stop teaching others the same thing.

This is how you break generational curses. You stop doing blindly what you have seen others do, and start learning and listening to God. God has something He wants you to do, but you will not do it if you're listening to somebody else. Many of us are under the spell and control of other people, rather than under the spell and control of Jesus. When certain people speak, like the rich man, everybody seems to listen and obey. But when the Word of God speaks, we turn a deaf ear.

We are like Balaam who was on the ass and couldn't see that God was trying to get him to change directions.[3] We are like Eli the priest and his sons Hophni and Phinehas – we are right in church and can't hear God talking.[4] If you want to put a stop to any curses in your life, you must first learn to hear and obey the voice of God.

If you have to make a break with your family – don't be afraid to part with them, for Jesus said in Matthew 16:26, *"For what is a man profited, if he shall gain the whole world, and lose his own soul?"* I wouldn't let anybody get in the way of me going to Heaven.

Somebody that you buried in the past died under that generational curse and they are praying for this generation. They want you to change directions. You can hear them speaking through this unnamed man in Scripture. If they could come back and tell you face to face that they were wrong – they would – but it's not permitted.

The only witness God is sending you is the Holy Bible. Abraham said in verses 29 and 31 that the only warning you will get is from *"Moses and the Prophets."* In other words, the only voice you ought to obey comes from God's Word.

If God's Word is not greater than the word of some of your relatives, then you can't be a child of God. A child of God will always obey his parent. I don't know who it is and I don't know what it is, but God is trying to tell somebody that his or her days are getting shorter.

God is telling you your shadow is growing longer, your steps are growing shorter, and your hair is a lot grayer. Somebody in the deepest Hell is praying that you will make it to the highest Heaven.

Prayer
Lord, please help me to see where I may be overly influenced by people who are pulling me away from you. Help me to surrender to you only. Show me where family and church tradition have kept me from having a true

relationship with you. Please help me to study your Word and to hear your voice. In Jesus' name – AMEN

[1] Luke 3:16
[2] John 3:7
[3] Numbers 22:26
[4] 1st Samuel 2:12-17

2

The Ghetto Gospel

Galatians 1:6-10 – *I marvel that ye are so soon removed from Him that called you into the grace of Christ unto another gospel:*
Which is not another; but there be some that trouble you, and would pervert the gospel of Christ.
But though we, or an angel from heaven, preach any other gospel unto you than that which we have preached unto you, let him be accursed.
As we said before, so say I now again, If any man preach any other gospel unto you than that ye have received, let him be accursed.
For do I now persuade men, or God? Or do I seek to please men? For if I yet pleased men, I should not be the servant of Christ.

"I don't know of any man who can turn down oral sex," the deacon blurted out. I could not believe my ears. I had to look over at Deacon Sandles to make sure I had heard correctly. Judging by the startled look on his face, I had heard just fine.

We were questioning a Deacon from a neighboring church about an alleged affair with one of our married members. Rather than deny the charges, this man, a deacon no less, proudly stated what he had done. He thought he was just fine because in his mind the woman, our member, had seduced HIM. He was actually stating that HE was the victim.

Upon speaking to his Pastor, I found the same sentiment: the deacon was seduced on several occasions by the same woman. "Deacon Jamerson has been called to preach and he is running from his calling," the neighboring pastor told me with a sympathetic shrug. It was hard to reconcile the fact that a man who would run from a godly calling would actually run toward deadly sin.

I could not find any sympathy in the Scriptures for an unrepentant person who practically stated that no man can resist sexual temptation. Hence, the Deacon did not get any sympathy from me. I read Galatians 1:8-9 and chalked it up as another person who is sadly deluded while sitting in church under a pastor who is preaching a "Ghetto Gospel."

Between 1968 and 1973, theologian and author Clarence Jordan wrote a series of books collectively known as the "Cotton Patch" Gospel. Jordan's goal was to translate the New Testament into the social context of the South, so that "plain folks" could better understand it. Although Jordan had a degree from the University of Georgia in Agriculture and a PhD in New Testament Greek from the Southern Baptist Theological Seminary, he chose to live in a rural area among poor blacks and whites.

In 1942, Jordan started an interracial, farming community of Christians in Americus, GA. This community was called Koinonia Farms. *Koinonia* was chosen as the name of the community because it is the

Greek word for "fellowship." Jordan's goal was to lead men and women to Christ. His tool was the Holy Bible.

When he would preach, he would translate his text to fit the settings of rural Georgia in the 1950's. For instance, he called Washington, D.C., "Rome". And everywhere in the New Testament where Rome was mentioned, he may have called it "Washington D.C." Since he lived in a time of racial segregation, if the word "Jew" appeared in a passage that he was preaching, he would say "white people" instead. If the word "Gentile" were in a passage, he would translate it "black people."

As he preached more and more, he became increasingly comfortable with his version of the Scriptures. His preaching was effective and responsible for saving many souls. In time, he found that he had taken whole books of the New Testament and made their settings fit that of the time in which he lived.

In fact, the founder of Habitat for Humanity, Millard Fuller, was deeply inspired by Jordan. He and his wife lived on Koinonia Farms observing Jordan for five years. Koinonia Farms was where the seed for today's Habitat for Humanity was planted. My point is that there is nothing wrong with preaching and teaching the Scriptures, so that the central message of the Gospel is made relevant to the day and time in which we live.

Yet, there is a grave danger when one attempts to do what Clarence Jordan did without sufficient training. In today's Church, we have a group of men and women who don't preach the "Cotton Patch" Gospel or the King James Version of the Gospel, but rather have perverted the message of the Holy Bible to be little more than a "Ghetto Gospel."

Clarence Jordan changed the setting of Scripture to fit his day and age. He did it without changing the essential meaning of Scripture. The "Ghetto Gospel" is not really a version of Scriptures, but I give it that name because it is a form of the Gospel that is directed primarily toward those who are poor, under-educated and more likely than not – a racial minority.

The Ghetto Gospel is not easy to spot, because it's not a lie that you can spot immediately. You and I know when an outright lie is told. Paul didn't describe what was happening in Galatia as an outright lie; he described it in verse 7 as a "perversion" of the Gospel. A perversion of the gospel is a little more difficult to spot than an outright lie.

For example, if I promised that you could go to Heaven without confessing Christ, you would all know that I'm telling an outright lie. This is especially true if you see me confessing Christ each chance I get. I don't think anybody would fall for that lie. However, if I told you that you could attend church, but stay in sin and still go to Heaven, some of you may be tempted to believe this lie; especially if you saw the preacher committing the same sins as you and still getting up to preach on Sunday morning saying that he is on his way to heaven. This lie may not get everyone, but it will get some. For the ones who believed the lie, you will be mad with the preacher on Judgment Day, because only then will you find out that he lied.

In the same way, the Ghetto Gospel is difficult to spot sometimes; but when you finally figure it out, it makes you angry. This type of teaching would certainly make the Apostle Paul angry. In fact, Paul's letter to the churches of Galatia is commonly called his "angry" letter. It is called this because of Paul's apparent anger at the churches.

Paul knew these churches well. He planted many of them and labored mightily for their spiritual growth. But as soon as Paul left to travel to other places, false teachers came in and perverted what Paul had already taught. It wasn't an outright lie, but it would take time for the members to spot. The fact that the churches would fall for such teaching was difficult for Paul to understand and he was frustrated.

Paul wrote in Galatians 3:1, *"Oh foolish Galatians! Who hath bewitched you..."* Paul couldn't understand why the churches he had taught fell for such trickery so soon after he left. The Ghetto Gospel has entered many of our churches, and there are very few who recognize it for what it is. As an example, some of our members have heard it said by both pastors and deacons of other churches, that it is okay to frequent the casinos for the Bible does not speak against it. There is a church in a nearby city that used to gather its members on the church bus and make the hour-long drive to Vicksburg to gamble. Truthfully, many of those who share our pews on Sundays, also frequent the floating units.

True, the word "gambling" does not appear in the King James Version of Scripture. But just like Paul warned the Galatians, we ought to have been taught enough in *other* parts of Scripture to know that anything that damages families and relationships is morally wrong.

The Gentiles in the churches of Galatia could have used the same argument; "Paul, the Bible doesn't speak against circumcision or observing Jewish religious practices – rather it encourages it." Paul would probably answer, "Yes, but these practices were put in place only to get you ready to meet Jesus. Now that Jesus has come, rituals such as circumcision are obsolete." There was some truth to their argument, but it was still a lie. This is what makes the Ghetto Gospel so dangerous.

In our communities, churches don't generally speak out against gambling, even though there is a high correlation between gambling and poverty. A study by the National Institute of Mental Health concluded that in 1989, 4.2 million Americans were addicted to gambling, 60 percent of whom had yearly incomes under $25,000.

Playing craps on the sidewalk is illegal; but when it's done down on the boat where the wealthy men who own the boat can prosper and the state can tax it, *then* it's legal. Just because something is legal doesn't mean that it is also ethical. Only those who preach and live a ghetto gospel can support gambling.

The Gospel message is under attack by those who prosper from the suffering of the poor. We have pulpit pimps in our churches that are determined to remove holiness from the cultural landscape and substitute rabid promiscuity in its place. They are not telling outright lies, in some cases, but yet, they are perverting the truth by supporting a Ghetto Gospel.

Shacking, sex outside of marriage, homosexuality, lesbianism, and bisexuality are all-available under the Ghetto Gospel. They are not regularly condemned, because they have become such a part of our everyday lives. Everybody knows somebody who is practicing sexual perversion on the "down low." Again, no outright lie is being told, but the truth is being perverted.

The truth is that these lifestyles are deviations from Scripture and ought to be condemned by the Church. But because the Ghetto Gospel has encouraged these lifestyles, even among the clergy, AIDS/HIV is rampant in our communities. There are some sitting in our churches today, who have AIDS/HIV and don't even know it.

There is a new outbreak of syphilis and other STD's in our communities, and we don't seem to be alarmed. The lie is not apparent on the surface. On the face of it, churches seem to be doing well. But look at the lives of the members. The proof is in the details. We don't see the connection between our leaving the *Holy* God, the *Holy* Bible and the *Holy* Spirit and our depressed state.

Holiness has become a thing of the past in many of our churches. We don't even think about holiness anymore. A friend of mine who is a pastor was invited to speak at a men's conference sponsored by a local church. He was told that his text should be based on Biblical manhood. Before he got up to speak, he witnessed the singing of several male choruses. While he sat there preparing to speak, he noticed that some of the choirs had directors who were openly homosexual. There was no *outright* lie told in the service, but there *was* a perversion of the truth.

Like Paul, it really does make one wonder whether somebody has cast a spell on us. Some of my fellow clergymen of the Gospel refuse to speak out. They are afraid that they will lose their pulpits. Paul faced this very *same* issue. He was educated enough *in* the Gospel to know when he heard a perversion *of* the Gospel. He risked his life to expose the lie.

Paul was viciously attacked. There were some who said that Paul was not even a real apostle. They said the apostles in Jerusalem – especially Peter and James - were the real preachers. They said Paul had no authority, because he had not gone through these men. Furthermore, they said that Paul was making it easy for the Gentiles to be accepted in God's Church. In response, Paul asked a rhetorical question in Galatians 1:10, *"For do I now persuade men, or God? Or do I seek to please men? For if I yet pleased men, I should not be the servant of Christ."*

The Ghetto Gospel seeks to please the people rather than God. People flock to a perversion. People will come from far and wide to go to Heaven and still live like Hell. There were some hard things that Paul had to say to the churches of Galatia in order to get them back to Christ. They had allowed lies to enter the church and Paul risked everything to set the record straight.

Our churches are running the same risk spiritually as those churches in Galatia. There is nothing wrong with applying Biblical truth to everyday life and clothing it in the vernacular of a particular community. But if in our attempt to make the Gospel relevant, we have to change its meaning, then we have lost the truth.

We have men and women who don't know Greek from Hebrew, yet, they take great liberty in how they preach God's Word. Clarence Jordan used the truth of the Gospel to change the Segregated South. Our way to improving the inner city is through the truth of the Gospel - not by changing the Gospel to reflect life in the inner city.

We don't "trick out" the Gospel like we trick out a car. We don't "pimp" the Gospel like we would pimp our rides. Our teaching about the truth of Jesus Christ has been corrupted. In its place, we have been given a "Ghetto Gospel" which in the words of Galatians 1:6-7 is *"no gospel at all."* In a community where 7 out of 10 births are out of wedlock, loose living cannot be taught or exemplified in the church.

We cannot glorify saggin' pants, ear-rings, rap music, spinners and 20" rims. As Christians, we can't be for abortion. We can't be for divorce. We can't be in favor of living together when you are not married. We can't be in favor of revenge and getting even. These are all components of the Ghetto Gospel.

We cannot mix what the Masons, the Alphas, or the Deltas do with what God does. Paul taught the simplicity of the Gospel message. The Gospel, in Paul's thinking, could be summed up in two words "repentance" (a turning away from sin and turning toward God) and "faith" (a belief in the God that I cannot see). This was all that was needed to receive God's forgiveness and the gift of new life.

The biggest problem with the Ghetto Gospel is that it doesn't save. It will never change people's lives from the inside out. Paul said in Romans 1:16 that the Gospel is "the *power of God unto salvation to everyone that believeth...*" If you are tired of living ghetto fabulous, God can change you. If you are tired of the boat and the club scene, the gospel is the power of God unto salvation to everyone that believes.

Jesus, the Son of God, came in the flesh, lived a sinless life, died on a cross one Friday evening for our sins. Sunday morning, sometime before dawn, He rose from the grave by the regenerating power of the Holy Ghost. He's now at the right hand of the Father interceding for us. If you believe this in your heart and can confess with your mouth, you will be saved.

Prayer

Lord, give me the spirit to discern false teaching from the truth. Help me to know that your way of doing things do not change with the times. Give me the guidance I need to stay away from those who pervert your Word and pull it down to meet the world's standards. Lord, please give me a hearing heart so that I may respond to your true Word and be transformed by it. In Jesus' Name - AMEN.

3

What Happens to the Family When the Mother Talks to a Snake?

Genesis 3:1-6 – *Now the serpent was more subtil than any beast of the field which the Lord God had made. And he said unto the woman, Yea, hath God said, Ye shall not eat of every tree of the garden?*

And the woman said unto the serpent, We may eat of the fruit of the trees of the garden:

But of the fruit of the tree which is in the midst of the garden, God hath said, Ye shall not eat of it, neither shall ye touch it, lest ye die.

And the serpent said unto the woman, Ye shall not surely die:

For God doth know that in the day ye eat thereof, then your eyes shall be opened, and ye shall be as gods, knowing good and evil.

And when the woman saw that the tree was good for food, and that it was pleasant to the eyes, and a tree to be desired to make one wise, she took of the fruit thereof, and did eat, and gave also unto her husband with her; and he did eat.

"Pastor, I have some bad news," Tammie said. "What is it, sister," I replied. "Well, I'm not a gossip, but the girl we took in today…" "Yes, go on," I encouraged her. "She is having an affair. I see her and her….LOVER all the time." I was actually relieved.

"Pastor, this is serious and you're smiling," Tammie glared. "Sister, she confessed everything at the altar – including the affair. She told me how she had no intention of committing adultery, but was drawn into it by his smooth conversation." "I see him all the time,

Pastor. He thinks he is quite the ladies man, but I know he is just a snake. Pastor, you're smiling again!"

"Yes Sister, it was also a snake that almost destroyed the first family in Genesis chapter 3," I said as we ended the conversation. "Let's thank God for opening Tiffany's eyes so she could see the snake for who he really is – Satan. Let's also thank God for her husband, Rufus, who stood by her."

Much has been written about the opening chapters of the Bible. Usually the preaching or writing on these verses is of a lofty and sublime nature. The Garden of Eden in its entire splendor has been described eloquently. And some of the writing regarding the tenants of this garden has been some of the most moving literature ever produced. The picture is this: nature at its highest and man at his highest.

Yet, when this particular passage, Genesis 3:1-6, is analyzed and stripped down to its bare essentials, it becomes nothing more than a conversation between a woman and a Snake about forbidden fruit. This passage is a part of what has been termed "primeval history" which means that it under-girds *all* history.

It does not matter whether you are black, white or Asian. It does not matter whether you live in Europe or the deserts of North Africa, the claims of Genesis 3:1-6 affects all of humanity. Anyone who has ever been in love or wanted something that was not theirs is drawn into the central message of these verses.

In the opening verse, we are introduced to a creature that heretofore had not been mentioned: the serpent. To really understand the central message, we must first understand the serpent. The Hebrew word for snake or serpent is *nachash,* which means to hiss or whisper as in whispering or chanting a magic spell. Now some theologians believe that because the snake was cursed in Genesis 3:14 to crawl upon its belly, that when he spoke to Eve he was standing upright. This upright snake was said to "hiss" or whisper and could be very seductive.

When a woman talks to a snake, she is naturally attracted to the snake. This attraction is due to the snake's unusual nature. He is a peculiar creature. He walks upright and, although he may not necessarily be beautiful, he does possess a certain appeal that makes him seductive. In some cultures, the snake is a symbol of sex and fertility. Before a man opens his mouth, a woman knows whether or not she is attracted to him sexually.

In addition to the serpent's appeal, the Bible describes him in verse 1 as being the most "*crafty*" of all the beasts of the field that the Lord God had made. The word "*subtil*" or "*crafty*" in the Hebrew tongue is `*aruwm,* which means "*cunning*" in the bad way that we use the word cunning. It also has the idea of "smoothness" or "slickness." So when we say that someone is "slick" or "smooth" the idea of the serpent is implied. Not only does the snake have sex appeal to the woman, when he opens his mouth, he is naturally smooth in what he says.

Evidently, the snake was endowed with the gift of speech for he spoke to Eve in eloquent terms. Not only was he capable of speech, he also was capable of reasoning for he *reasoned* with Eve. So whatever we think of snakes, this was no ordinary snake in the way that we think of snakes. Eve's reaction to the snake, lets us know that she was not surprised that he walked upright, that he talked, was able to reason, and was fairly charming and probably good looking.

Yet, we are called to remember that the snake was still an animal. And God gave dominion over the animals to man in Genesis 1:28. Eve should have exercised her dominion over the snake – but she didn't. Mother's should exercise their discretion over a man who is not their husband.

I've asked women on certain occasions, "What were you thinking when you broke up your home for this snake?" They usually tell me about how the snake talked them into certain things. They'd had some dealings with the snake and they did not see his cunningness as a threat. He literally talked them into things that they never thought they would do.

In the same vein, I've heard snakes brag about their conquests and exactly how they conquered the mothers of little children. It involved becoming friendly with the woman and then looking good and talking good.

Having a little power or position also helps the snake to win somebody's mother. When a woman meets a snake, she is already enchanted before he opens his mouth and begins to reel her in. Let us turn now to the nature of the woman to discern why she is especially vulnerable to the serpent.

Now we know that the woman is no match for the snake because in the last verse of chapter two, Moses gives us the key to the whole encounter. Moses writes in Genesis 2:25, that the man and woman, the father and mother, were both naked. The word "naked" in the Hebrew is *arowm,* which is the *same* word for "*subtil*" or "*crafty*" in 3:1. The writer is saying that Eve didn't know the games that the snake would play, and so the snake would use his power because Eve was naïve to the game.

The serpent knows Eve's weaknesses. The majority of African-American women in this country are unmarried with children. This means that they are trying to support families on one paycheck. Without a man, there is no mechanic in the house when the car breaks down. Without a man, there is no security guard for when things go "bump" in the night. Without a man, there is no one to talk to you when you get lonely or to hold you when you are feeling vulnerable. The serpent knows how to manipulate the single woman in the very places where she is weakest.

The serpent tempts married women as well. It doesn't matter to the serpent. Any woman who somehow feels that she is not getting what she needs at home is vulnerable to the serpent. And the serpent is always seeking through his 'serpent knowledge' to find a woman who is willing to play his game.

It's not as if the woman doesn't know that what the snake suggests is bad for her, because she does. Eve knows that she is a good girl. Eve was married to Adam. In fact, she was *made* for Adam. God brought Adam and Eve together in the first marriage. Eve knows what is right. We may surmise that Adam has told Eve what is right, because she repeats what Adam has said in her conversation with the snake. It's funny how a married woman will repeat intimate details of her life with her husband to someone outside the marriage.

Obviously, Eve has spent time talking to the snake. In Genesis 3:1 when the snake says, *"Yea, hath God said ye shall not eat of every tree of the Garden?"* it seems to be a continuation of a conversation that they previously had.

The snake didn't just walk up and seduce Eve; he probably had been carrying on conversations with her for some time. This is why women have to be careful about conversing with men who are not their husbands. Eve had been talking to the snake on a casual level. In fact, most of the sinful things that we end up doing started with some talk. The sin that placed all of humanity under a curse and nearly broke up the first family was only one verse long – verse 6. Yet, verses 1-5 were all the conversation that took place. Women generally love to talk and snakes love to listen and look for their opening.

The snake chose his time carefully because he was smooth and cunning. He knew that Eve was a good girl who knew God's law. Perhaps he waited until a day when he sensed an opening. Ladies, if you are upset with what is going on in your home, you should know that you are especially vulnerable to snakes. These snakes probably have been around you seeking the time that they can exploit you. There obviously has been some friendly conversation that the snake was using to build Eve's trust.

When the snake gets Eve's trust, his whole desire is to make her doubt. If the snake can get Eve to doubt what she knows in her heart to be right, he then can get her to act in a way that is really against her self-interest. No mother or wife really wants to break up her home or anyone else's. Yet, if the serpent can get you confused about what is right, you become easy game. After all, the serpent is smooth, good-looking and walks upright like he is respectable.

The snake will give a woman a reason to doubt that what she has at home is good. The snake will give the woman a reason to not be good. "Well, he's doing it." "Everybody's got somebody on the side." "He just doesn't appreciate you." "Does he really make you happy?" Remember the snake is not only good-looking, but he is very seductive and chooses his words and timing very carefully. If you watch carefully, every now and then, he will stick his tongue out – just like a snake.

The snake is trying to remove Eve's inhibitions. He does this in small steps. He catches her on a day when she is probably feeling more vulnerable; he then comes up to her all good looking and begins his smooth talk. Remember that the serpent's tongue is forked, so that when he speaks his voice probably has a magical quality. He is only an animal, yet Satan has given him the capacity to reason and also speak. Satan speaks to Eve through the Snake.

The snake doesn't begin with anything big; rather, he continues a conversation they had earlier. "Really? Did God say *none* of the fruit in the garden? God says you must not eat any of it?" Notice that the snake doesn't attack the truthfulness of God, at first. He merely tests Eve to see what she is thinking. Remember, the snake is cunning. Eve said they could eat the fruit of the trees of the Garden, except that fruit from the tree in the middle of the Garden. *"We can't eat it or even touch it,"* she said.

This was undoubtedly a conversation that Eve should not have had. Women should not talk to snakes – period – unless it is due to their job. If someone on your job begins to come between you and your husband – you need to find another job. There should be *no* discussion on this point. Eve thought she could handle the serpent just as some of the Pentecostals in the hills of the Carolinas believe that they can handle serpents – yet eventually, everyone gets bitten. Mothers and women, you are no match for the serpent.

Secondly, Eve is talking about fruit from a tree that God has forbidden them to eat. There are certain conversations that married women should not have with men who are not their husbands. Married women should *never* talk about sex or money with men who are not their husbands. These subjects are taboo. Whatever problems there are in your home, those problems should *never* be discussed with men or women outside of the home, unless it is with your pastor or a marriage counselor.

It does not matter how long you have known a person. Some conversations are off limits, once you become married. Some friends you should lose the very minute you say, "I do." Some women and some men have been talking to snakes all of their lives and are afraid to break the connection. The charming serpent would probably have pretended to be heartbroken had Eve stopped the conversation. The snake *knew* Eve had a tender heart and he played on it.

Much worse, once he got Eve to talking, Eve herself talks about the law of God in a reckless way: "E*at* off the tree, we can't even *touch* it!" "Go *see* my male friends? I have to *sneak* to call them on the phone." Now the serpent knows that he has gotten her. She has shown some discontent with being good. Of all the things that she could have and did have, she was focused on the *one* thing she didn't. Women, the snake's job is to search for the *one* thing. Once he finds the *one* thing, he has got an opening.

In verse 4, the snake shows his true colors: "That's a lie," the serpent hissed, "*You will not surely die.*" The snake is now defying what the woman *knows* to be good. Eve was a good woman who loved Adam and loved God. She was talking to a no-good snake that used his charms to find the one thing and when he found it, he jumped on it.

He wanted to make Eve feel like God wasn't giving her His best; that somehow, God was holding back on her. "*God knows very well that the instant when you eat it, you will become just like him, for your eyes will be opened and you will be able to distinguish good from evil.*"

The snake promises things that he can never deliver on. Snakes are big liars. In this case, the snake promises wisdom and higher knowledge, which would lead to freedom. No woman likes to feel in bondage to somebody else – even if that somebody else is God Himself. Women are naturally freedom-loving people. The snake offers women a few hours freedom from the kids; the snake offers career advancement; the snake offers excitement of the variety that you can't get at home. All you have to do, is what Eve did, forget what you know to be right and start focusing on what you *don't* have.

Most affairs start with "What I don't have" or "What I'm not getting." Can you see the snake, sticking out his forked tongue at Eve? Eve now sees the snake for what he is – a destroyer. The snake says plainly that God is wrong. A snake will attempt to get a woman to lie with him; even though she knows it's wrong.

He will tell her that it's all right and that her feelings about doing the right thing are really wrong. The snake promises more, but *always* delivers less. When a woman talks to a snake, the situation is always to her detriment and the detriment of her kids and her husband. Yet, Eve and the woman ultimately have a choice to make. Things don't just happen, they happen when we choose for them to happen.

Finally, the snake pulled his trump card; he showed Eve the tree. The tree represents the greener pastures on the other side of the fence. The tree represents the happiness that you think you don't have. The tree represents the solution to your every problem. The tree represents everything that you think you don't have. The tree will make you whole. The tree will help you live happily ever after.

As a result of the Mother talking to the snake, she and the Father got put out of their home. They lived in a wonderful home, but because of the disruption caused by the snake – they lost the home. How many times have we seen couples' living in nice homes and then the tempter comes and they lose it all? Because Eve talked to the serpent, Adam and Eve got put out of their home and sent to a lesser home (Genesis 3:22-24).

Adam and Eve managed to stay together, which is more than we can say for most couples, but their marriage was now one based on mistrust. Adam exercised his iron will over Eve because he no longer trusted her. God cursed the relationship because the woman talked to a snake. She went from being an equal partner in marriage to being a servant of the man (Genesis 3:16).

This is why there is no trust in many marriages; men share a common memory of our wives talking to snakes. We remember the hurt we felt when the woman stepped out on us with a snake. So now, we have one eye on every snake that comes around and the other eye on our wives. The old serpent was exposed for what he was: an animal that crawls around on his belly trying to hurt people.

The only way back into the home that was once filled with love is through forgiveness. Forgiveness only comes through Jesus Christ. Husband and wife must both return to Him and He will repair the relationship. He will heal what the snake tried to destroy.

Prayer

Lord, I know I'm wrong. Please help me to see and understand that any man who would cause me to break my vows is not from you. Have mercy on me and bring me to true repentance so that I may serve you free from guilt and sin. In Jesus' Name – AMEN

4

What Happens to the Family When the Father is Absent?

Genesis 3:1-6 – *Now the serpent was more subtil than any beast of the field which the Lord God had made. And he said unto the woman, Yea, hath God said, Ye shall not eat of every tree of the garden?*

And the woman said unto the serpent, We may eat of the fruit of the trees of the garden:

But of the fruit of the tree which is in the midst of the garden, God hath said, Ye shall not eat of it, neither shall ye touch it, lest ye die.

And the serpent said unto the woman, Ye shall not surely die:

For God doth know that in the day ye eat thereof, then your eyes shall be opened, and ye shall be as gods, knowing good and evil.

And when the woman saw that the tree was good for food, and that it was pleasant to the eyes, and a tree to be desired to make one wise, she took of the fruit thereof, and did eat, and gave also unto her husband with her; and he did eat.

"Gene, you gotta be stone crazy," I said. "Why, John?" Gene said looking confused. "Because man, you wonder why your daughter stays out in the streets with every Tom, Dick and Harry; you wonder why your wife curses her out and they both curse you out. Can't you see it? Your family is messed up because you are messed up!" I was screaming at the top of my lungs, but at least Gene seemed to be listening.

"So, you're saying that it's my fault," Gene said looking astounded. "How long have you been with your wife?" I asked. "Ten years married and another five before we got married," Gene said. "Now," I reasoned, "how long have you been faithful to her?" "John, I pay the bills and put food on the table…" I stopped him right there and said, "I do the same thing for my dog. Gene, you've got to come out of the streets and be the father and husband God is calling you to be. Your cheating ways show up all over your family."

"How can I get control of them again?" he asked sadly. "Gene, you gotta repent and let the Lord get control of YOU. God has a special task for men," I said reaching for my Bible. "Let's start with what got us in this predicament – Genesis 3:1-6."

The thing that we notice *immediately* in this passage is that the Father is either absent or silent. Eve, Adam's wife, is in danger. She is talking to a snake. Some not so erstwhile scholars have suggested that Eve or the woman was the downfall of the human race. Such a view is simplistic, misogynistic and not in good keeping with the overall tenor of Scripture. True, the woman was no match for the serpent, but also the man was missing in action.

Previously, we talked about "What Happens to the Family When the Mother Talks to a Snake?" and now, we want to examine "What Happens to the Family When the Father is Absent?" We are looking at the same passage from two different perspectives. Previously, we looked at the woman in all of her dealings and conversations with the snake. Now, we examine the man's role in the Garden of Eden in light of his absence in the contemporary family.

I'm sure that you have all heard the statistics. Almost 70 percent of black children are born to single mothers. These mothers are far more likely than married mothers to be poor. They are also more likely to pass that poverty on to their children.

The African-American community is crippled because of poverty. For decades we have blamed others, and others have done their parts to keep us down, but at some point, we have to stop looking at others and start looking at ourselves. The "man" did not cause me to make a baby and not marry its mother. The "man" did not cause me to repeat my first mistake over and over and over again with different women.

These children, my children whom I did not raise, will grow up and repeat the same cycle with the same results. For those of you who are math scholars, the more this cycle repeats the deeper the ditch that Black America is in. The same is true for the woman, the "man" did not make you, as a young woman, have four or five children with different daddies that you can't afford to raise properly.

This situation may be the only reality for those who live in secular Black America, but for those who have been saved this is not the pattern that God has set forth for the family. For those of you who claim the name of Christ, this passage in Genesis is instructive.

First of all, it teaches us that the Father is a co-laborer. He must be with his family – working alongside the mother. There is no godly reason for most black men to live away from one or more of their children. God intended for Adam to be there with Eve. This is what a co-laborer is. This couple is described as being 'one-flesh.' As Eve was talking to the snake, Adam's presence is not felt. I'm not one to read into the text what is not there, but I sometimes wonder would the outcome have been different if Adam would have kept more company with Eve.

Most men are good at bringing home the bacon, but we have to come home with it. Taking care of home is never good enough. The home needs the presence of the husband and father. I know that God intends for the Father to provide for the family, but the first order of business is to be present in the home – with the family. Some Fathers believe that they can run two or three different homes and raise two or three different children in different locations. This is neither biblical, nor possible.

Men, if you are going to celebrate the fourth of July, celebrate it in the house with your children and your wife. If you want to celebrate Labor Day, stay at home with your family and celebrate. No husband should be away from his wife's side during the holidays or tipping around during the year.

Some men are just like Adam – we are not around. We may keep our shoes under the bed and our toothbrush there, but we spend nights away from the home. Some men tip away a couple of nights a week. This is no good – your presence is required in the home. I had a good friend who worked the night shift. He worked all night and left his family at home. I told him that this is not good and that he should find another job. He didn't. Within five years, he was divorced. The man first and foremost ought to be with his family – especially at night.

Other men, for whatever reason, are not in the home at all. They send checks and then they complain. They complain to the Mother about how she is raising their children. They complain about all the bad things in the child's life, but they forget that as Fathers they have broken the first rule – they are not present in the home. Talking about what would have happened if we were there is just like talking about what would have happened if Adam were there for Eve. It's useless talk, because the fact is, Adam was not there for Eve.

God Himself, in Genesis 3:9, *"...called unto Adam, and said unto him, Where art thou?"* If you have left your children, God is asking you, *"Where are you?"* In other words, Adam - you are not where you ought to be – which is where I placed you. God places the man at the head of the Family. When we get out of place, that absence is felt in the family.

Secondly, this passage teaches us that a father is a carrier of the Word of God. A saved Father is the carrier of God's law. When God's law was given in the Garden, it was given to Adam – the Father who was made in the moral image of God. Genesis 2:16 reads in part, "*God commanded the man...*" The Hebrew word for "commanded" in this verse is tsavah, which has several meanings – one of which is to "set in order." The command was given to Adam that the Garden was to be set in order.

The order for living in the Garden was that Adam and his family could eat from any tree with the exception of the tree of the knowledge of good and evil. Adam and his family were also responsible for the care of the garden. If Adam could keep the garden in order, he would please God. So Adam was not only present in the garden, he was responsible for making sure that the garden operated in such a way that would please God. This is what God told Adam in Genesis 2:15-17.

Fathers are not born with the law, just as Adam was not born with the law. Men must be instructed from the Word of God as to their responsibilities. Men must be saved in order to please God, then they must be taught what God expects. A man should be present in Sunday school, worship service, Brotherhood and other activities in order to learn what God expects from him. A man is not fit to run a house unless he has learned proper order.

Ignorance is no excuse, for the man is responsible, in God's eyes, for the order of the home. If he is not there in the home, he cannot ensure its good order. If he is present in the home, he is charged with operating it in a manner that will please God. This is why Satan wants the man out of the conversation with the woman in chapter 3. If you were getting ready to tell somebody wrong, would you want the preacher around? The man, as the priest of the home, is not addressed because he *knows* the law.

Satan does not address the man at all. His usual pattern when dealing with married people is to always address the woman. 1st Timothy 2:14 reads, *"Adam was not deceived but the woman being deceived..."* Satan will talk to a woman in order to turn her against her husband. Paul said in 2nd Timothy 3:6 that *"weak women are led astray..."*

Why? Because the man is hard-wired for the truth – God made him that way. Satan knows that the man, by his very nature is wired to please God. Oftentimes, the man does not have the complexities of a woman. His mind generally works in terms of black and white; right and wrong; left and right. When the mind of a man is made up – it's pretty hard to change. God made him that way because he is the primary bearer of God's law – which does not change. James said in James 1:8 that *"a double-minded man is unstable in all his ways."* God's man is firm because God's law is firm.

The Father sets the course for the family. When he says "green," the color *will* be green. The woman is more complex. She then chooses whether it will be olive green, teal green, forest green or yellow green. The man is responsible for setting the course. Without a saved

Father, Satan knows that the moral course of the family is not set properly.

It has been **well** documented that without the Father present in the home, African-American males are pre-disposed to fail in school, go to jail, be poor and/or die early. But before the African-American male dies, he starts the cycle all over again by having babies and then not being in the same house to 'father' them. This is just secular fathering.

Men, you cannot be a good father without knowing Christ. If you are not saved, statistically, you are less likely to marry the woman who has borne your children. I hear all the time about how we men take care of our children by spending time with them and sending checks. That is not good enough. What our children need is for us to be married to their mothers. Married people make plans for the future: they save, they invest, they hope, they dream, and they teach values. Our children see this and learn from it. When the Father is not present, there is no structure, no hopes, no dreams, and no values being taught.

And men, if you are married, don't be like Adam, who if he was present, was silent. If you are saved and you have the truth within you – your family needs to know the truth. God put you there to be man enough to tell them the truth. Statistics reveal that if the father is saved, the entire family is more likely to be saved than if only the mother was saved. The same holds true for church attendance. If the father attends church, he is more likely to require that everyone under his roof attend church. This is not so with the mother.

Men, sometimes our silence in the home has deadly consequences. I don't know what Eve may have done to alienate Adam. Perhaps it was all the time that she spent talking to the snake or maybe Adam was just a moody man. The minute that Eve misquoted God in verse 3, Adam should have corrected her, because he was the carrier of the Word. We learn from Adam, that whatever the source of our anger or silence, we must remember that we are the head and our anger affects not only us, but also the entire family.

I've heard it said that if mother is not happy, then nobody is happy. But we, as African-Americans need to pay special attention to the Father's silent sulking. This silent sulking has an impact on the family. Fathers, when we see things going wrong, we need to remember that we are the embodiment of the law and not saying anything or saying the wrong thing is just as bad as not being there.

Mother may do a decent job with the family, but she is not wired to provide the structure or the law that a family needs. Why is Mother not wired to do it? Because the father is the corrector of those who break the law.

My third point is that the Father is a corrector. His job is to correct those in the home who break God's law. The law of God is firmly implanted in the Father, because he is endowed with the physical presence to enforce it. There is no need in making laws if there is not a means to enforce them. God intends to enforce His law through male leadership. We would all agree that the physical make-up of men and women is different. *Generally*, men can lift more, lift longer, and lift higher than women. Women may know where something fits best, but the man's job is to lift it and make sure it gets there.

The male species was endowed with great strength and power to enforce the law of God. We don't mean to imply that a woman is not capable of enforcing the law. But what we want to make clear is that in God's way of doing things - enforcement is something that the Father is responsible for. Mother may be able to curse, threaten and perhaps swing a belt a few times like the Father. Yet testosterone, in the case of the raising of the Black male, must be met head on and redirected into something positive.

Black males can't really point to their fathers and say, "I saw his pants saggin'." Because in all likelihood, those who have fathers at home are not allowed to leave the house with their pants sagging. They know that a black man in the home is an enforcer and if they get caught with their pants sagging, Daddy will put a belt on their behinds and then around their waists. Men teach boys how to obey.

When black males don't learn how to obey at home, they end up in the criminal justice system. Fathers, if you don't stay at home to be a daddy to your boys, the State or the Federal government has an "institutional daddy." It was set up to father all the black males whose fathers don't do their jobs in correcting their children.

In the case of the black female child, if daddy is not present to give her the love she needs from a male perspective; she will reach out to the boys of her age – not looking for sex, but looking for love. But because she has not learned what love is versus what lust is, she will perhaps end up pregnant and the cycle will begin again. Our girls are not as bad as we make them seem; they are just looking for a man outside the home, because they don't have a father in the home to provide some order.

They need a law-enforcer to come in and say, "pull your skirt down below your knees." They need a law enforcer to say, "get back in the house and cover your cleavage." When girls leave a home where the Father is present, the Father knows that his girl represents him.

You can tell when a little girl doesn't have a daddy at home; she has low self-esteem and is always in a boy's face at school trying to get attention. These girls don't know anything about love and self-acceptance, because they haven't seen it at home. Again, I am not faulting the mother, but God says that it takes two to raise children properly and the man's role of correcting is missing in our families.

Those girls with Fathers at home spend time with their daddies and don't need the validation of a man outside the home. When it's time for these girls to get married, they know what love is because they have seen it in their father – a black male who stayed home with their mother when he could have been running the streets with a mistress or with another family.

When the law was broken in the Garden, God called Adam to account. He didn't call Eve or the serpent – he called Adam. God gave Adam the law and charged Adam with keeping the garden in order. We can't say with a straight face that we are all right with God when we are not in right relationship with our family.

If you have children who were not raised in the home with you, you did not do what you were called to do as a Christian man. It doesn't matter if you sent checks or what the mother was like. If you spent time making the child, you who are responsible for correcting in the house, need some correction.

Fourth and finally, the Father is a conductor. He stabilizes the family. Like it or not, men were made to be levelheaded. Again, I am not saying that women cannot think clearly. I am saying that men are less emotional and more physical. Our physical nature is tied up with our testosterone levels. Remember, men are wired to think in simple terms and often act based on the facts and not any emotion.

Women, on the other hand, are wired to be emotional. It is in the estrogen. Wives will do things out of extreme emotion and make some Fathers mad. Adam had to be mad at Eve. When God asked Adam about the trouble in the family, Adam quickly blamed Eve. Eve had spent all that time talking to the snake in Genesis 3. The snake almost busted up Adam's family.

Adam could have done what most men do – leave and find a snake of his own to talk to, but he didn't. Adam stayed with Eve even though they had to leave their home and times got rough. Even though women may do some things that harm men, God gave men staying power. A woman will waffle over whether or not to leave a man. She will change her mind a million times and continuously second-guess herself.

But when that man makes his mind up to leave, he's gone and generally he is not coming back. It is this quality that makes men conductors. Men have to learn to stay home no matter what and make that family what God intended for it to be. Our families have failed, because we men have failed. We have failed to be the co-laborers, carriers, correctors and conductors. Father's put the "F" in family.

Just as a backbone holds up a body, a Father holds up a family. If you want to see love, watch a black man, his wife and his children. Our leadership and broad backs is what holds the family together and gives it its structure. Without structure, the family will disintegrate into chaos; "stepmothers" and "step-daddies" along with "play uncles" and "play cousins." This family structure will never work. The snake brought all these things into being because of the absence of the Father.

No matter what we think about it, no lesbian can take the place of a Father in a woman's life. No boyfriend can take the place of a Father. No grandmother or mother can take the place of a Father. When things get rough, a boyfriend has the option to leave, but a Father was put in the family to make the family stable. If a Father doesn't learn anything else, he ought to learn to stay at home and stay in position. Adam was out of position and the enemy was successful. If Adam had stayed home, the snake would not have had a chance.

Men, there are snakes waiting for you to leave home so they can slither in. You think nobody wants your wife after you have left her poor and with children, but snakes will slide in – take the fruit – and then slide on out. All the while, your children are sitting there watching.

A man can take a lot more than a woman, if he will wake up and realize who and what God has called him to be. God called Adam to be the head. The head is responsible for making sure that everything else works properly. When you are the leader, you can expect adversity. You can expect to be beat down by the enemy. The enemy wants you to leave. The enemy wants you to sit around sulking and complaining. The more you do that, the less time you spend structuring and organizing.

The tallest pine tree in the forest is the one that takes all of the lightning strikes when a thunderstorm moves in.

Men, God made you to be that tree and you ought to stand up strong and straight and be who God wants you to be. Our children don't need more government programs - they need more of us.

Prayer

Lord, show me how to be a husband and father to my family. Teach me submission to your will and your way. Show me how my obedience to you affects all the relationships in my family. Forgive me for falling and failing my family. Now help me get up and stand as a man. In Jesus' Name - AMEN.

5

When Wrong Seems Right

1st Samuel 25:39 – *And when David heard that Nabal was dead, he said, Blessed be the Lord, that hath pleaded the cause of my reproach from the hand of Nabal, and hath kept His servant from evil: for the Lord hath returned the wickedness of Nabal upon his own head. And David sent and communed with Abigail, to take her to him to wife.*

Sheila was in her element. Her glass of Chardonnay was held high and with her free hand she gave her sorority sign. As her long hair hung down over her shoulders, the men nearby watched as she danced provocatively.

"I'm thinking about giving it all up," Sandra thought as she watched her friend Shelia dance. "This is too much for me: another sorority party, another one night hook up, another hangover and another guilt trip in the morning." As she pondered these thoughts in her head, Rico came over and asked her to dance. "Here it goes," she thought, "another drunk frat looking for an open pair of legs."

"This is all wrong," Sandra said over the loud music. Rico replied, "But it seems so right." Sandra pulled away and thought about the passage of Scripture she'd heard last Sunday in church; "What was it? Oh yes, 1st Samuel 25:39 – *'When Wrong Seems Right.'"*

There are times in life when wrong just seems right. There are men and women who are against having sex outside of marriage. In fact, most of us in church would be against sex outside of marriage. This is well and good, but when you find yourself involved with somebody who is not your husband or wife, it seems so right. You know it's point blank wrong in God's eyes, but we have every excuse for continuing to do wrong. Wrong then seems to be right. Every other person who is in an adulterous relationship is wrong – except us.

Many of us would agree that bad language is wrong. But let the right thing happen to us and we will gladly use the worse kind of profanity. Wrong then seems right to us. There are times when we would never think of acting badly in church. But let somebody do us wrong and we'll tell them off and even get ready to fight right in the church. Then wrong seems right to us. There is no exception for wrong will seem right at some point in time – even to the 'so-called' best of us. This is where David finds himself in this passage of Scripture.

In the book of 1st Samuel, David has been anointed King, but Saul is still the de-facto King. Saul has heard that the Prophet Samuel has anointed David as the next King of Israel. David's appointment as King comes directly from God. 1st Samuel 13:14 reads that God sought out a man after his own heart to lead the Israelites. This man was David. Yet Saul, in his paranoia, has tried to have David killed on several occasions. David and a group of men – about 600 of them - who are loyal to him have spent years running and hiding from Saul.

David and his men lurked in deserts and in the wilderness. In their running and hiding, they had to depend on herdsmen and shepherds to feed them and provide them information on the whereabouts of King Saul. In exchange for food and supplies, David and his men would perform work for the shepherds and herdsmen. Sometimes they would even have to fight to protect them from bandits and outlaws. Undoubtedly, this is how David came to know Nabal and his wife Abigail.

This passage of Scripture is set in a very festive time of the year. It is the spring and the sheep are ready to be sheared. The shearing of the sheep was a large operation and evidently had become sort of like a festival: there is plenty of food and merriment to go around. This was a time when neighbors would share with other neighbors and everyone had something.

At this time of year, Nabal, whose name means "fool", was shearing his sheep. He had three thousand sheep which would have made him a very wealthy man. Not only had the Lord blessed him materially, but he was married to Abigail, whom the Bible describes in 1st Samuel 25:3 as being very beautiful and intelligent. When David heard that Nabal was shearing his sheep, he sent ten of his young men to Carmel with the message that the Bible gives us in 1st Samuel 25:7-8.

The passage is as follows: *"And now I have heard that thou hast shearers: now thy shepherds which were with us, we hurt them not, neither was there ought missing unto them, all the while they were in Carmel. Ask thy young men, and they will shew thee. Wherefore let the young men find favour in thine eyes: for we come in a good day: give, I pray thee, whatsoever cometh to thine hand unto thy servants, and to thy son David."*

David's request seems honest enough. It is at the time of the year that the shepherds have brought the flocks in to be sheared and there is plenty of good food and entertainment. It was common to share with your neighbors at this time of year. David's servants spoke humbly and even said, "please" according to the custom of the day.

Yet the fool gives his answer in 1st Samuel 25:10-11: *"Who is David? And who is the son of Jesse? There be many servants now a days that break away every man from his master. Shall I then take my bread, and my water, and my flesh that I have killed for my shearers, and give it unto men, who I know not whence they be?"*

This is the equivalent of you doing something kind for somebody and then asking him or her to return the favor in a small way and they tell you to 'get lost.' When David got the message from his men in verse 13 – he said *"Gird ye on every man his sword."* David took four hundred of his men and started off to kill Nabal and all of his servants. Now wrong seems right to David at this point.

Many of us have been disrespected in our lives. This is how murders begin even in our time. It begins with some perceived slight such as "he was looking too long at my woman;" "he owes me $20;" "she talks down to me." Many of us men are just like David, we have good hearts, but we are too eager to pay folks back for some perceived wrong – even though it seems like the right thing to do.

Nabal was a fool and he did the wrong thing in how he answered David. He could have told him "no" in a polite manner, but his words and his tone were such that David felt like he had to respond. Somehow, his honor had been offended.

There is nothing wrong with this. At some point in our lives, someone will offend our honor. There is a line that we believe that we cannot cross. When it happens, we need somebody to help us. In verse 14, we find that there was a servant who was listening to the conversation between David's servants and Nabal. Notice that the servant did not go to Nabal.

The servant could have gone to Nabal and said "Brother you messed that up." But Nabal, in all likelihood, would not have listened to a servant. If he treated David's servants that badly, you can imagine how he would have treated his own servant.

The servant goes to Nabal's wife – Abigail. He tells her everything in verses 14-16. The servant tells Abigail how David's men were good to them in the wilderness. He even describes them as a *'wall of protection that was up day and night'* in verse 16. He concludes in verse 17 by telling Abigail: *"Now therefore know and consider what thou wilt do; for evil is determined against our master, and against all his household: for he is such a son of Belial, that a man cannot speak to him."*

When there is trouble someone must be the intercessor. If no one had gotten involved, David would have killed this man and his entire family. In verses 21-22 the Bible reads that *"Now David had said, Surely in vain have I kept all that this fellow hath in the wilderness, so that nothing was missed of all that pertained unto him: and he hath requited me evil for good. So and more also do God unto the enemies of David, if I leave of all that pertain to him by the morning light any that pisseth against the wall."*

When we have been wronged, our worse nature comes out. David thought about all that he had done for this man and received nothing in return, but insults. Some of us have done some good things and all life has seemed to give us is bad things – so we then revert to our lower nature in order to take what we believe we have earned. Some of us believe we are not being paid fairly, so what our employer doesn't pay us, we justify by stealing –whether it's stealing time on long lunches or stealing money or merchandise. This is when wrong seems right. You cannot justify wrong no matter what the situation is.

When you cheat on your taxes; when you lie to get a new car or even to get your credit cleaned up; wrong is never right. We believe we are owed something just like David, but in reality, life owes us nothing. We are not entitled to anything other than what God will give us. Some of us say we have been mistreated at home, so we go outside of our marriage looking for entertainment. Pastors have hurt some of us and our hurt is legitimate, but getting back at him or the church is not the right answer. This is when wrong just seems right. What we need to help us to see this - is an Abigail.

Abigail came to David when his anger was at a boiling point. She didn't go with head high and shoulders pinned back like the wealthy woman she was. Verse 23 reads, *"And when Abigail saw David, she hasted, and lighted off the ass, and fell before David on her face, and bowed herself to the ground."* This is similar to Paul's teaching in Galatians 6:1 where he says *"Brethren, if a man be overtaken in a fault,* [make no mistake about it, David is now overcome by sin], *ye which are spiritual, restore such an one in the spirit of meekness; considering thyself, lest thou also be tempted."* When a person is in sin and doing wrong, we can't sit still, but we have to have the right spirit when we approach them.

Abigail said in verses 24-26 *"...Upon me, my lord, upon me let this iniquity be: and let thine handmaid, I pray thee, speak in thine audience, and hear the words of thine handmaid. Let not my lord, I pray thee, regard this man of Belial, even Nabal: for as his name is, so is he; Nabal is his name, and folly is with him: but I thine handmaid saw not the young men of my lord, whom thou didst send. Now therefore, my lord, as the Lord liveth, and as thy soul liveth, seeing the Lord had withholden thee from coming to shed blood, and from avenging thyself with thine own hand, now let thine enemies, and they that seek evil to my lord, be as Nabal."*

Abigail wasn't even there and yet she is taking the blame. When God sends His children to intercede in conflict, those who have clean records have to get dirty to keep the peace. It is not good enough for Christians to stand on the sidelines, while injustice is being done. We must get involved. First, there was the servant who got involved. The servant went to Abigail because he knew she could fix it.

When Abigail gets involved not only does she fix it, but she also takes the blame for it. Sometimes when there is conflict, even if we are not the blame, we have to take the blame in order to bring people together. This is what Paul was doing when he interceded in a conflict between a slave named Onesimus and his master named Philemon. Paul told Philemon in Philemon 1:18-19, *"If he hath wronged thee, or oweth thee ought, put that on mine account; I Paul have written it with mine own hand, I will repay it..."*

When wrong is being perpetuated and it's going to end up in further hostilities, Christians have a duty to get involved, not only in word, but in deed. God is trying to use Christians who are sitting on sidelines and will not get involved. David recognized that Abigail was sent from God to intercede. He said in verses 32 and 33: *"...Blessed be the Lord God of Israel, which sent thee this day to meet me: And blessed be thy advice, and blessed be thou, which hast kept me this day from coming to shed blood, and from avenging myself with mine own hand."*

Some of us are a party to broken relationships. We see the adultery. We see the alcoholism and drug-abuse. We see the materialism and striving after things that don't belong to us. We see the kids failing in school and going down the wrong path. Yet, we will not say a word. We know that many of the things we see in our families are wrong, but we don't open our mouths. We just wait until something bad happens and then say, "I told you so."

God is calling for Christians in the community and in the church that when you see wrong, you intercede. Take the blame yourself, if you have to. Sacrifice yourself in order to hold the body together. It doesn't matter who was wrong and who was right – just hold the body together. The body might be a family. The body might be a church. The body may even be a community. If there are intercessors, it can be held together.

There was a time when Christians were not Christians. We were wrong, but we thought we were right. God the Father was just like David. He came to us and told us of all the good things that He had done. He told us about how He protected us and kept us when we couldn't keep ourselves.

All He asked was for a little time and a little of our treasure. What we said to Him by our actions was a shame and a disgrace. We said that we will not come to Bible Study or Sunday school – it takes up too much time and they are not talking about anything.

We said that we would not give ten percent – that's too much. We said that we will not pray and read our Bibles – it takes too much time. God the Father was mad at sinners. He wanted to give us justice, which was Hell.

Along came Jesus – who was our Abigail - to intercede on our behalf. He went to the Father and pleaded our case. He won our peace and reconciled us to the Father!

__Prayer__

Lord, I pray that you will show me all the areas in my life where I am doing wrong, but the wrong seems right. I acknowledge that what I may think or feel is of no consequence. Help me, O Lord to discern your will for my life and help me submit to it. Cleanse me, O Lord, for I know sometimes wrong seems right. In Jesus' Name – AMEN

6

What Will It Take For You to Repent?

Come now, and let us reason together, saith the Lord: though your sins be as scarlet, they shall be as white as snow; though they be red like crimson, they shall be as wool. ***Isaiah 1:18***

Everybody knew "Git it Girl." "Pastor, I used to shut the clubs down. When I walked in, they knew I was going to turn it out!" Patricia was known in the local clubs as "Git it Girl" because of her dance moves and because she would fight at the drop of a hat.

She was loud and proud. She won contests all over the county with her display of the latest dance moves. Sometimes she traveled to several clubs in one night and would not come home until the wee hours of the morning.

"Pastor, that's the way I used to make my money." And she used to spend the money at the local casinos and liquor stores. In fact, most times you saw her she had a beer in one hand and a pack of cigarettes in the other. She was touchy and would kick, scratch, bite or cut a person – especially, if it was about her old man

Robert. Patricia and Robert had been living together in sin for over 20 years.

Robert had pimped, hustled, sold dope and used dope. He was known around town as "Shy Dog" because of his devilish ways. One day, Patricia and Robert were invited to church by her nephew, Tyrone, whom she affectionately calls "T-Man." Tyrone knew that Patricia and Robert were both unsaved and headed straight for Hell. They had been in and out of churches all their lives. Tyrone did not witness to them, but he sent them to a church where he knew the Pastor would condemn the lifestyle that they were living and then call them to repentance.

It took Patricia and Robert most of their adult lives, but they finally repented and accepted Jesus Christ as Savior. Patricia now turns the *church* out. She is one of the loudest and most emotional among the members. She is now known as "one-hundred percent," rather than "Git it Girl." "Pastor, I give Him one-hundred percent." She and Robert are married and serving in the local church - free from habitual sin.

As a Father, whenever I bring something new into our home, I always check all of the labels. I'm looking to see if what I have purchased could be a choking hazard, toxic, or otherwise hurt me or my family. I'm also looking to see whether batteries are included and whether I have all of the parts.

One day as I was unpacking a toy, I noticed a label that read 'for entertainment purposes only.' I laughed because what else would I do with the toy besides be entertained by it. Then I thought about all of the other places I had read the same disclaimer "for entertainment purposes only."

The Lord then laid His Church on my heart. Many church-goers have subconsciously labeled God's church as a place *"for entertainment purposes only."* Many of us come to be entertained rather than to worship God. The Pastor and the Choir are the principal entertainers in this thing we call church.

The choir is supposed to sing to uplift us. And the Pastor is supposed to preach to uplift us. The average church-goers are caught up in thinking that the choir is supposed to serenade them and the preacher is supposed to preach to their liking.

Yet if this is the case, then church is just for entertainment. When we desire to be entertained, then the worship service becomes about us. Yet, true Biblical worship is not at all about us – it is about God. When we can take the focus off of us and worship and praise Him, then we have really worshipped.

Worship is not something that you watch; worship is something that you do. You don't complain about the song you didn't like. You just worry about whether the song was pleasing to God. If I worried about whether my preaching was to your liking, I would be little more than an entertainer.

When it's merely entertainment, we don't expect anybody to be saved. There is not an appropriate level of seriousness to winning souls for Christ. In our preparation for services, we worry about everything but whether somebody will be saved. We worry about whether folks will like the song services and preachers wonder whether their sermons will be accepted.

But what we offer is not for entertainment purposes, it's for purposes of worship and winning souls to Christ. Our adulation and attention should be on Him – it's not about us.

How many of us have invited unsaved folks to our churches to get the Word? Everybody here has folks in our families and all around us who are not saved. Yet, we are not encouraging them to come. We say come hear this person preach or that person sing, but we don't say, "Come and meet Jesus."

When the attention starts to focus on us, then it's not acceptable to Him. We are coming to offer Him praises – not us. But in praising Him, it does uplift us because this is what we were made to do. We were made to praise Him and He should be the focal point of these services.

One of the greatest prophets who ever lived reserved some of his harshest criticisms for those who called themselves "God's people." By virtue of joining a church, you are pledging to live your life for Christ.

Many of us made our pledge as children and never really understood what it meant to serve God. Just as many Jews were born as Jews into a privileged, religious society, yet they never were converted in their hearts.

What God is looking for is conversion, or a changed heart, not more church members. This is the problem that Isaiah points out in chapter one of the book of Isaiah. He begins as if he is in a court of law and is attempting to prove the guilt of God's people.

In verse 2, he calls the heavens and the Earth to be his witnesses. They were called to witness two things: God's goodness and the rebellion of Israel against God.

God was good to Israel. Israel was a nation that was especially chosen by God. God gave them land, leaders and a legacy. Yet, they turned their backs on God by not keeping His commandments.

In the New Testament and in today's times, the Church is known as the people of God. God has also been good to us. We can rest assured of that fact by life itself. Only a good, loving God would even give us the gift of life. I believe we are all thankful for the opportunity to even exist.

Yet, we have rebelled against God because we refuse to become what He desires that we become. God desires that we give up on what we want and partake of His Spirit and become one with Him and with one another.

Isaiah points out in verse 3 that our rebellion is really due to a lack of understanding of who God is. Isaiah said that even animals know their masters, but the nation of Israel (the Church in today's era) did not know and did not understand God, who is her Master.

The examples Isaiah gave us were those of an ox and a donkey. An ox is an unusually stubborn animal; and in Bible times, a donkey was known for its stupidity.

Therefore, to say Israel (or the church in New Testament times) is less knowledgeable of God than an ox or a donkey is making a very strong statement about our stubborn stupidity. Some of us just don't know God. Others of us have some knowledge of Him, but we are just too stubborn to serve Him.

Isaiah didn't stop there; he said that these animals, the ox and the donkey, were more aware of their owners and the source of their sustenance than God's people. Israel did not know God or realize that He was her Provider. These are church people that God is addressing through Isaiah.

Isaiah calls nature to witness his case against God's people. We are not told of the crime that the people have committed until verse 4. The crime, of course, is sin. As the pastor, I don't define sin.

You may not like what I say to some of you, but I am merely repeating Scripture. Sin is anything that offends God. Sin is to know the law of God and then not keep it.

Because of sin, we stand guilty before God. This means all of us – from the pulpit to the backdoor. Romans 3:10 reads *"There is none righteous, no, not one."* I don't have to know your situation personally to know that you are guilty. The Word of God says that we all stand guilty before God.

The modern mind loves excuses. We say "sin" is not the problem. In the church, we say the Pastor is the problem. Yet the reason we can't get along with the Pastor is because of somebody's sin.

We say the Deacons are the problem. But the reason that we can't get along with the Deacons is because of somebody's sin. We say that we can't get along with Brother so and so or Sister so and so. The reason we can't is because of somebody's sin.

Outside the church, we say a one-parent home is the problem. But sin is the reason that it is a one-parent home. We say a lack of education is the problem. But institutional sin is the reason that we don't have quality educations.

We can blame the white man, the red man and any other man, until we recognize the sinful nature that dwells in us. God will not be satisfied with any of us, if we do not first examine ourselves.

Sin burdens the church. Isaiah describes the people in verse 4 as being burdened down with iniquity, a seed of evildoers, children that are corrupters, backsliders who have forsaken the ways of the Lord.

We wonder why we don't have any peace or why things don't go our way more often. It is because we have not acknowledged our participation in sin. We always say that it's the other person and not us. We even offer God excuses of why we can't do any better.

Isaiah says that in response to the sinful nature of God's people, He punished them. Isaiah recounted what was happening to Israel to help them understand that their difficult times had come because of their disobedience. In verses 5 and 6, Isaiah used the figure of a person who had been beaten and was bruised over his entire body.

God has allowed Satan to lift his hands against us because of our own disobedience. It is almost as if God is asking, *"What will it take for you to repent? I have taken your husband or your wife. I have used Satan to strike at your finances. I have given you a joyless existence in your heart."* What more will it take?

Verse 7 reads that the nation of Israel was beset on all sides by hostile forces and was losing territory to foreign nations. This was God's doing. They should have realized that these terrible problems had come because of their spiritual condition.

We have all kinds of suffering going on amongst our people and very few seem to be willing to say the problem may be due to the neglect of our spirituality. Almost 8 out of 10 new HIV/AIDS cases are black females.

There is a silent epidemic of STDs among our people. There is an over-representation of *us* behind bars. But we have not seen the worst yet. God is asking us, *"What will it take for us as a Church to turn around?"*

Isaiah describes God as the "Holy One of Israel." The Holy One of Israel has promised that He would destroy sin. If you think we have seen hard times, you better think again. These are good days compared to what will be unleashed before us.

All the while the nation of Israel was suffering, God's people were moving along as usual: gathering, bringing offerings, singing, preaching, teaching and then going home to commit more sin.

Isaiah said in Isaiah 1:13 that when the vast majority of God's people are in sin, the church meeting becomes a sinful one. Somebody ought to wake up and realize that God is not in it.

All of our singing, offering, praying, lifting of hands, and even preaching is in vain, if our hearts are not in it. It's the heart that God wants to change.

We come to church with the smell of the world still on us. Of course we bathe, but bathing will not remove the stench of sin from the inside. We come dressed up, but God is looking at the condition of our hearts. We come looking down on others. We get beside ourselves and thinking more highly about ourselves than we ought to think.

We come seeking to please men and women in the church, but not to please God. Our songs, our preaching, our praying and our playing of musical instruments mean nothing to God if they come from a corrupt heart.

Yet God is so good that He's still giving us a chance. Judgment has not been released in all of its fury. God is still having mercy. He asks in verse 18, "*Come now, and let us reason together; though your sins be as scarlet they shall be as white as snow.*" God says let us reason together. He wants to know, what it will take for you to come to Him.

What will it take for you to stop entertaining one another and start worshipping from the heart? What will it take for the churches to start being true churches of God? What will it take for you personally to repent?

Prayer

Heavenly Father, I now confess that I am a sinner - the lowest of the low. I have done many things that are against your will and your way. I realize that I cannot help myself nor can I cleanse myself. I need your help and the cleansing that is only found in the blood of your Son Jesus. Lord, please forgive me of my many sins and cleanse me from all unrighteousness. Come and live in my heart by the power of the Holy Ghost. Teach me your word and give me a spirit of obedience and humility that I may follow you and grow in your will and your way. Lead me to a church whose teachings will help me to grow more and more like you. Help me to forsake all sin as I now live for you. In Jesus' Name - AMEN.

7
Reflections on "The Fool"

"The Fool hath said in his heart, there is no God."
Psalm 14:1

"Be still and know that I am God: I will be exalted among the heathen, I will be exalted in the earth."
Psalm 46:10

It has been said many times that busyness is the enemy of spirituality. A life filled with the mundane: family, children, friends, work, church and school may initially appear to be a productive, Spirit-led life. Upon closer inspection, at either end of routinely long days, most people do not have time for spiritual matters. As a result, our lives are filled with activities that have no real aim: chores that do not have charity and goals that do not reflect God.

Of course, many of us attend church, serve in Parent Teacher Associations and support local civic organizations; yet in all of our serving and giving, we sometimes find that the chores have become our masters. Outwardly, we have lived up to images that are shaped more by our culture than by the very hand of God.

For instance, who could argue that "Joe", a hard-working blue collar engineer who married Susan his high school sweetheart and former cheerleader, who through grit and grace managed to put three girls through college, serve on various boards and still manage to teach Sunday school, is not a "good, Christian man"?

Yet, what if Joe never really knew what it meant to hear the voice of God or to feel His tender touch? What if he was only conditioned by his culture to respond in certain ways and had never bowed spiritually in humble submission and acknowledgement of his Maker? The Fool may be either the Sunday school teacher who never thinks deeply about the God she teaches, or the atheist who looks on in scorn at what he perceives is an exercise in futility.

The writings in this book are designed to challenge us to see if our inward reality of God is in sync with our external circumstances, and call us to take that initial step off the well traveled path, through the strait gate, and down the narrow way.

The narrow way begins with asking some tough questions. If you are ready to be honest with yourself, then I look forward to seeing you on this path. Your brothers and sisters in Christ are waiting for you on this narrow path.

Self Study

1. Has there ever been a time in your life when *"Wrong Seemed Right?"* How does one stay out of situations where being wrong seems right? What were some of the factors that were influencing you?

2. Have you spent time talking to someone and you knew the conversation was wrong? What were some of the factors that were influencing you? What steps have you taken to prevent these conversations in the future?

3. Do you believe that your individual life has purpose? What are your goals, dreams and aspirations? What makes you unique? Who, in your life, depends on you?

4. How much time do you spend in prayer? How much time do you spend thinking about spiritual matters? If you had to make a list of what you spend your time thinking about, would spiritual matters be near the top of the list?

5. What parts of your life get most of your attention but probably pull you further away from Christ?

6. Who have you pronounced judgment on even though you may be guilty of the very same thing? What do you think it will take for you to repent?

7. Have you been exposed to teaching that is unbiblical? Have you spent enough time in God's Word to know when a deception is being taught?

8. What are some things in your life that you know for certain are holding you back? Is the Lord first in your life? How do you know?

9. If an unbiased observer could observe your life as it stands now, are there some parts where your behavior could be characterized as spiritually foolish?

10. Is it possible for the Lord to grow you spiritually without you first confessing all your known sin and then acting upon the things that you know you ought to do according to the Word of God? If not, when will you confess and allow the Lord to grow you spiritually?

www.ingramcontent.com/pod-product-compliance
Lightning Source LLC
Chambersburg PA
CBHW051658090426
42736CB00013B/2438